Coloring book for adults and kids airplane image for design

This coloring bookis belongs to

....

....

....

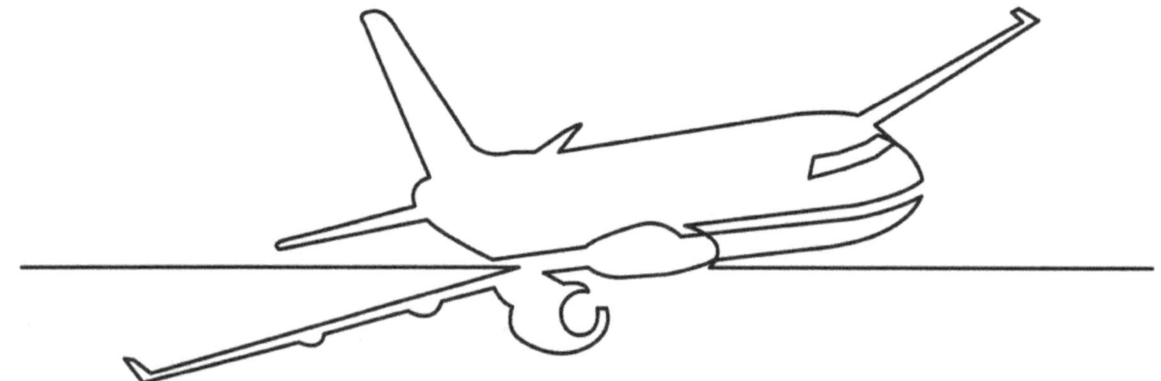

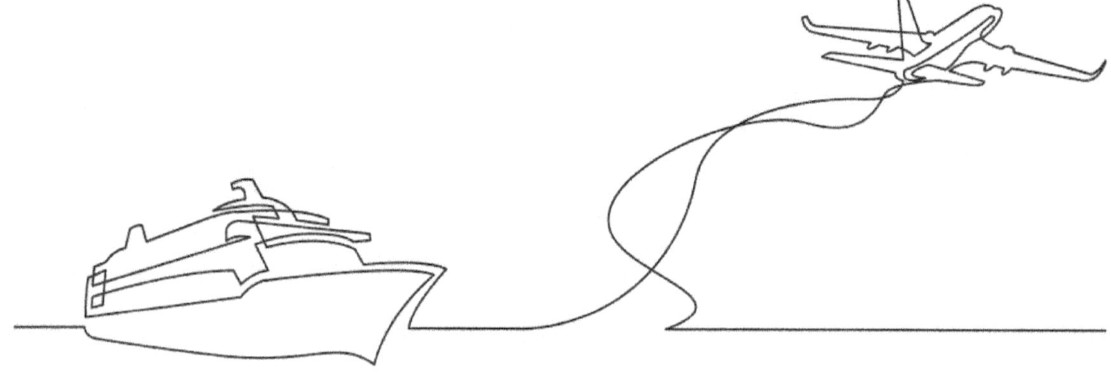

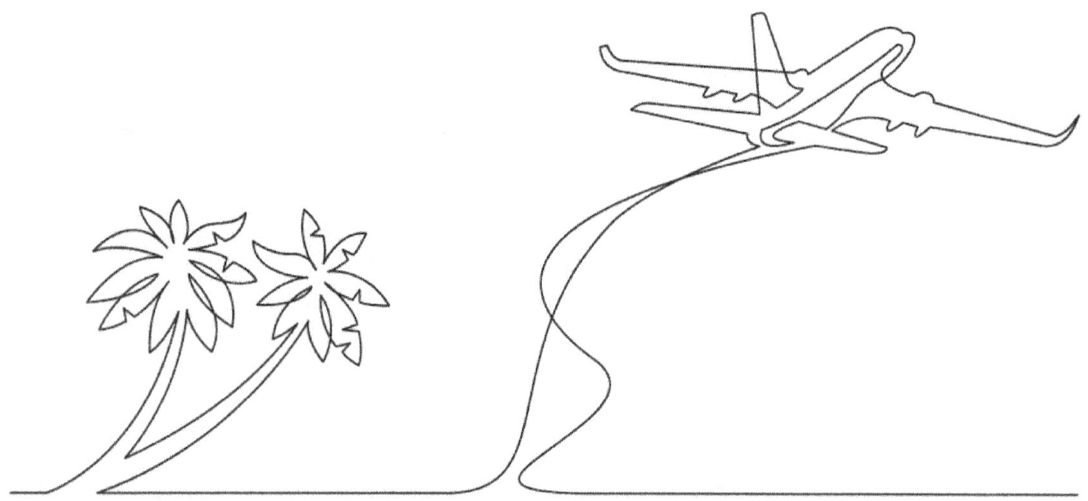

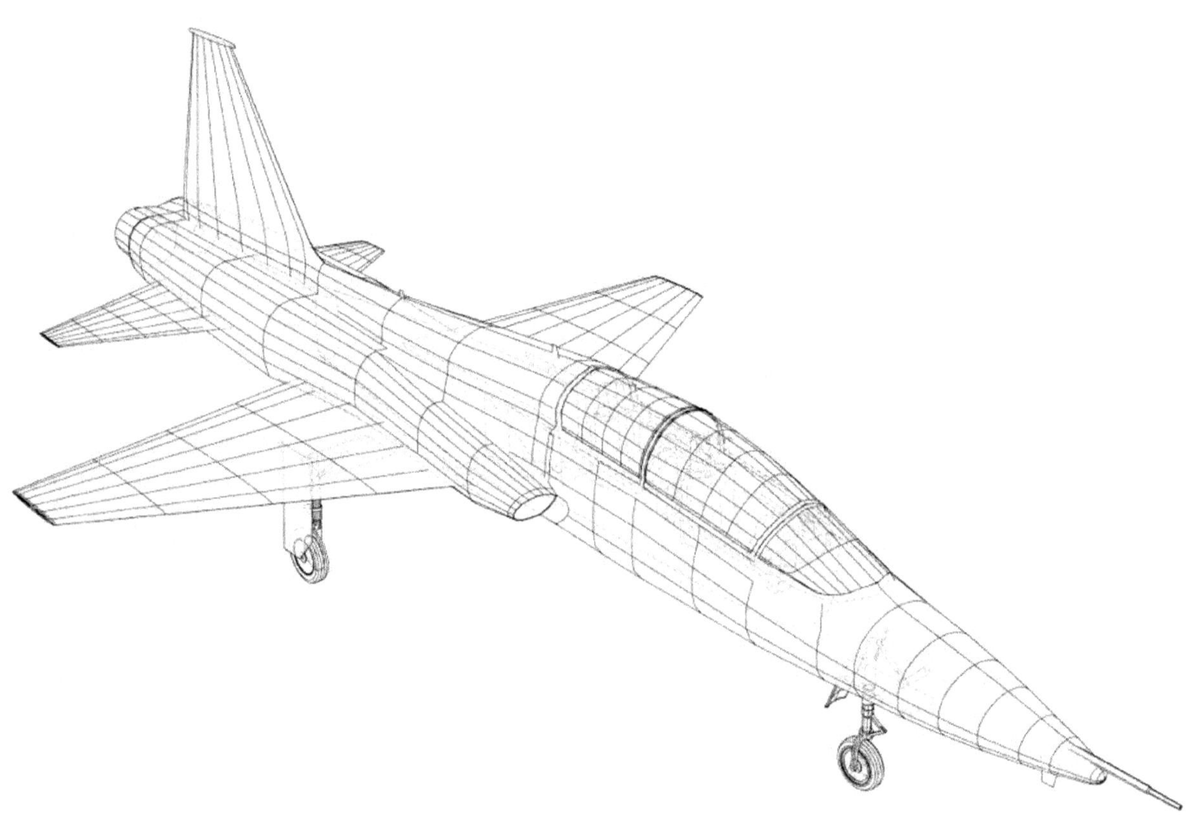

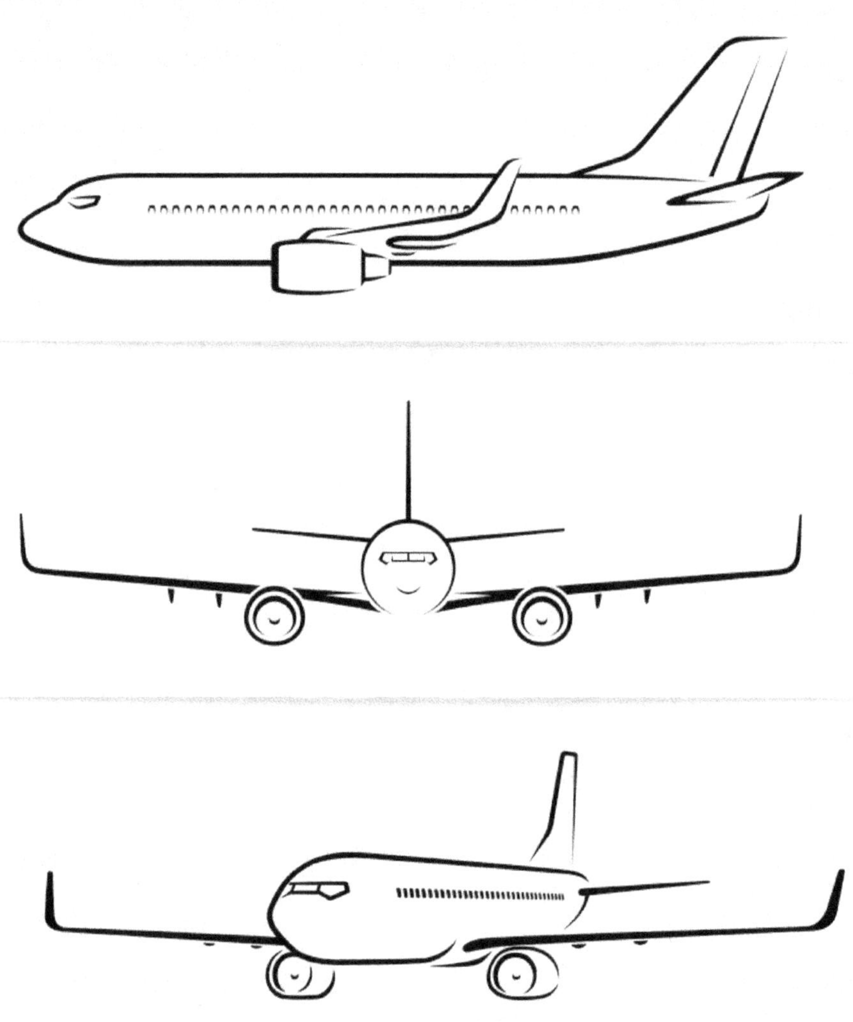

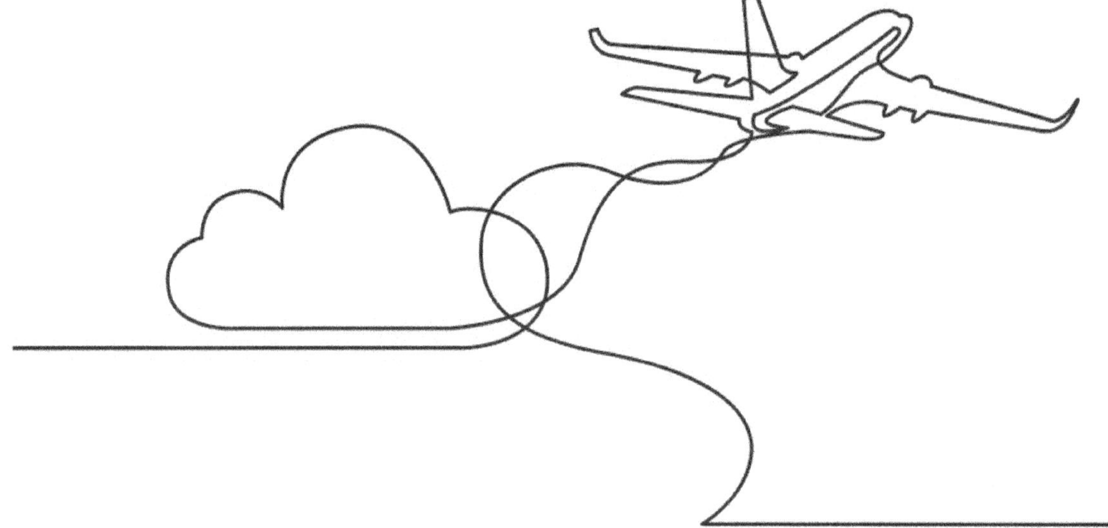

LET`S TRAVEL!

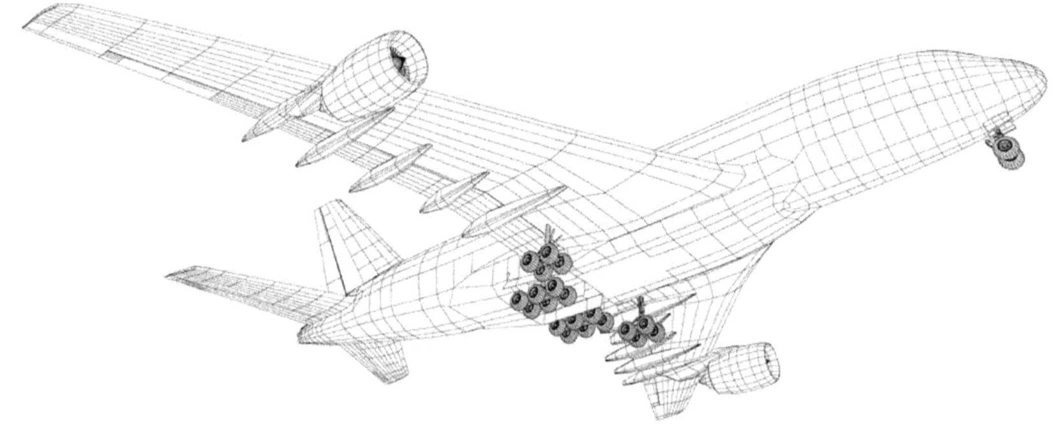

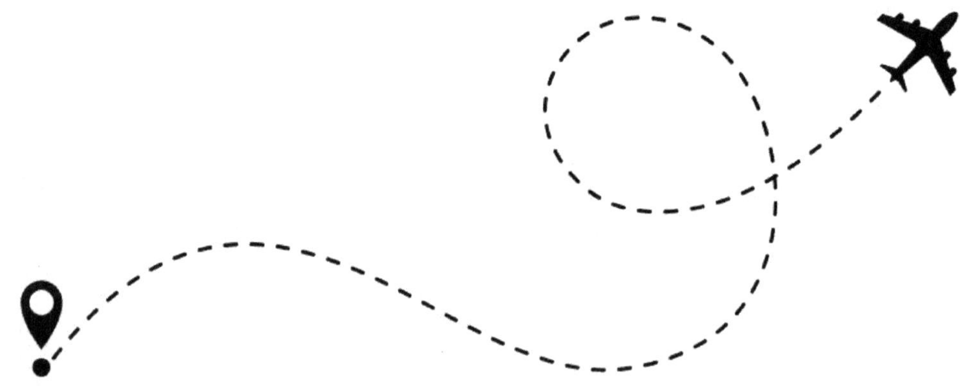

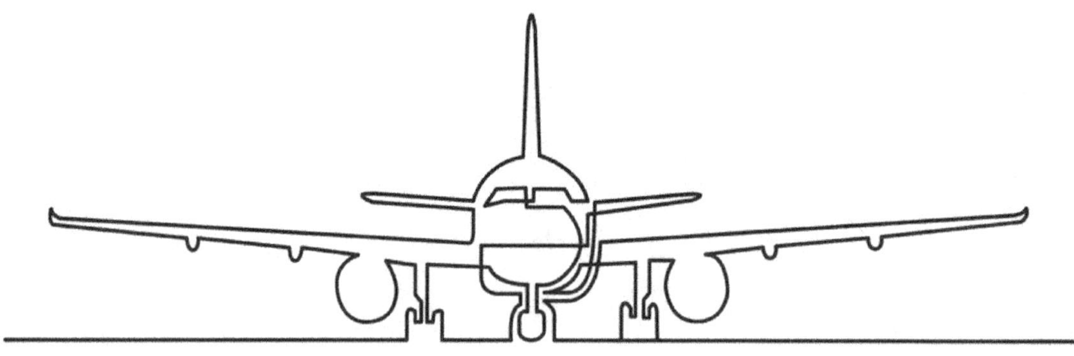

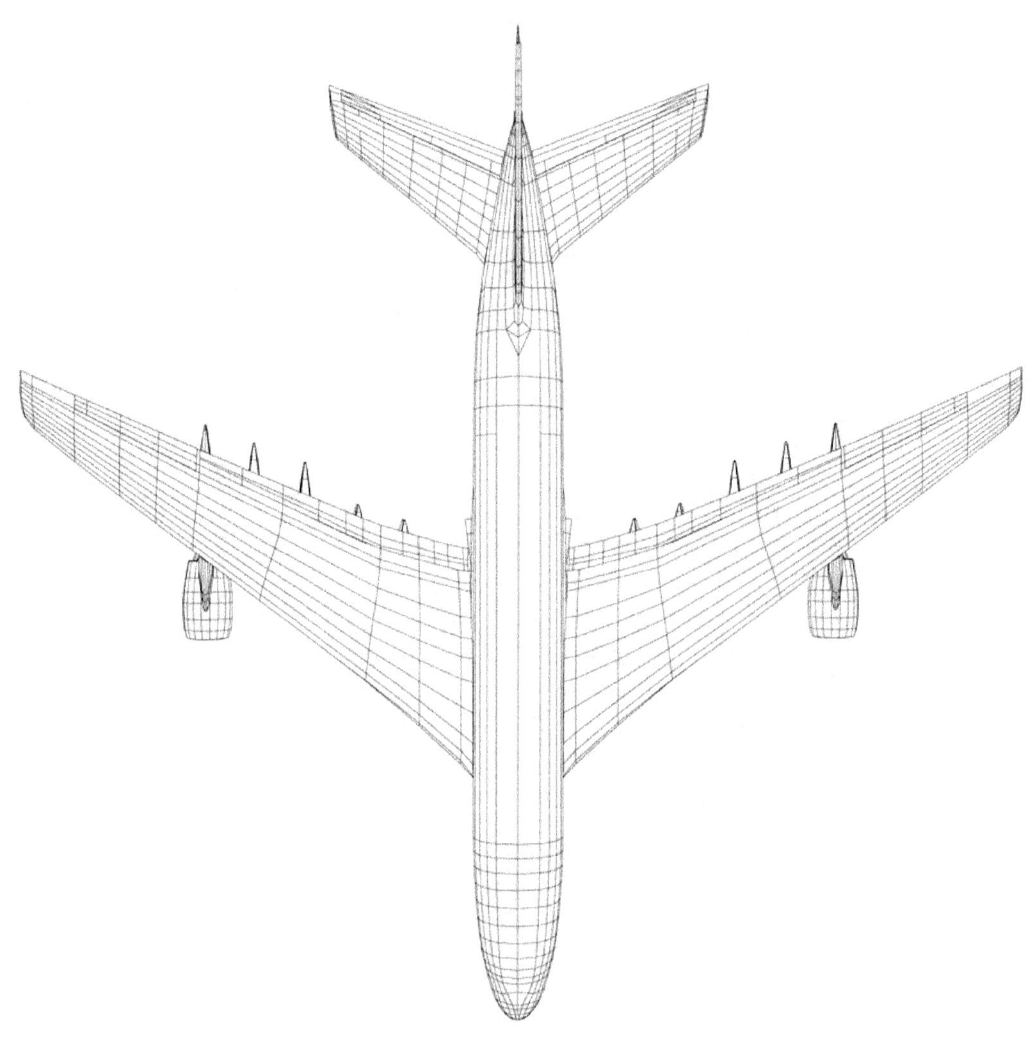

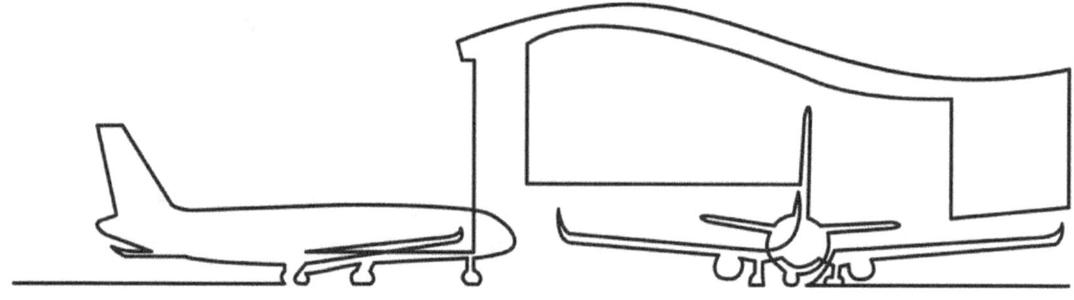

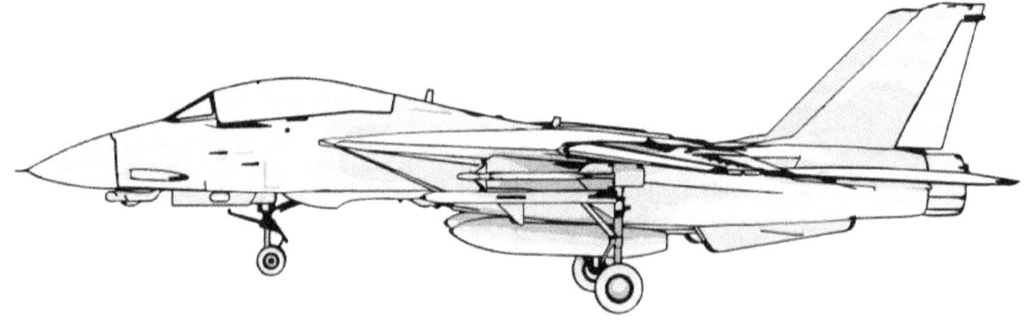

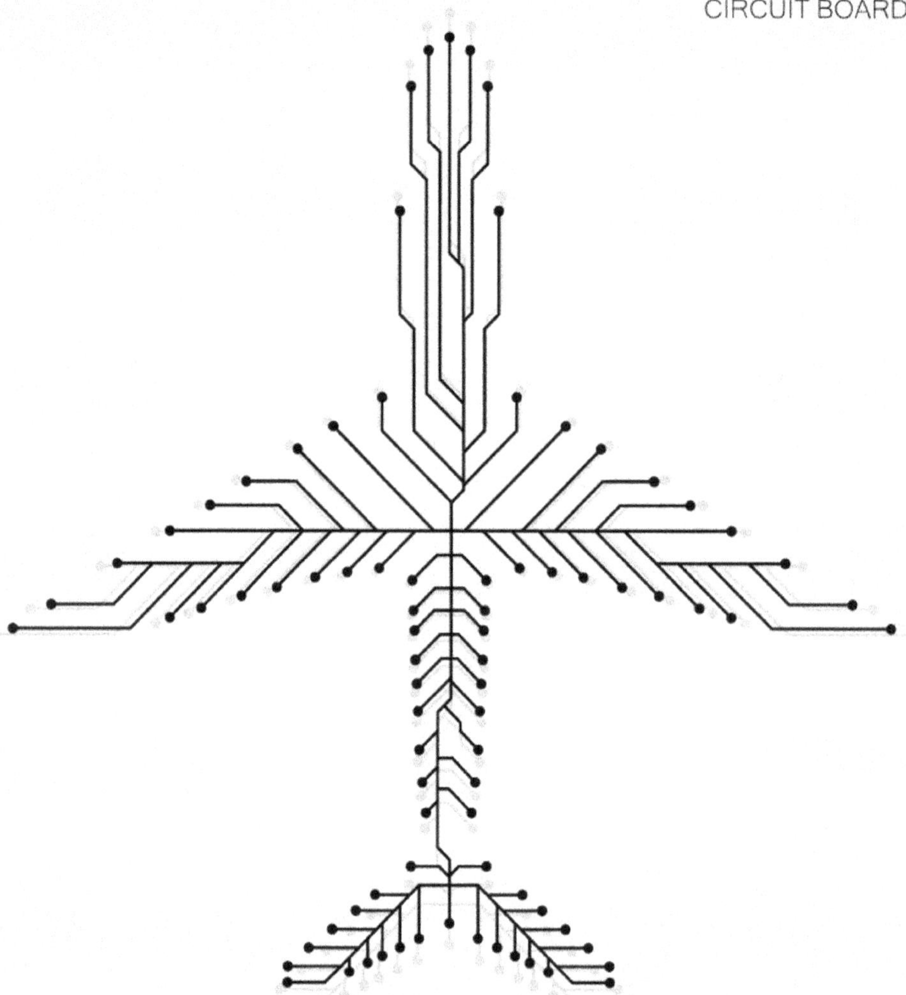

ABSTRACTAIRPLANE
CIRCUIT BOARDVECTOR

be happy

AiRPORT

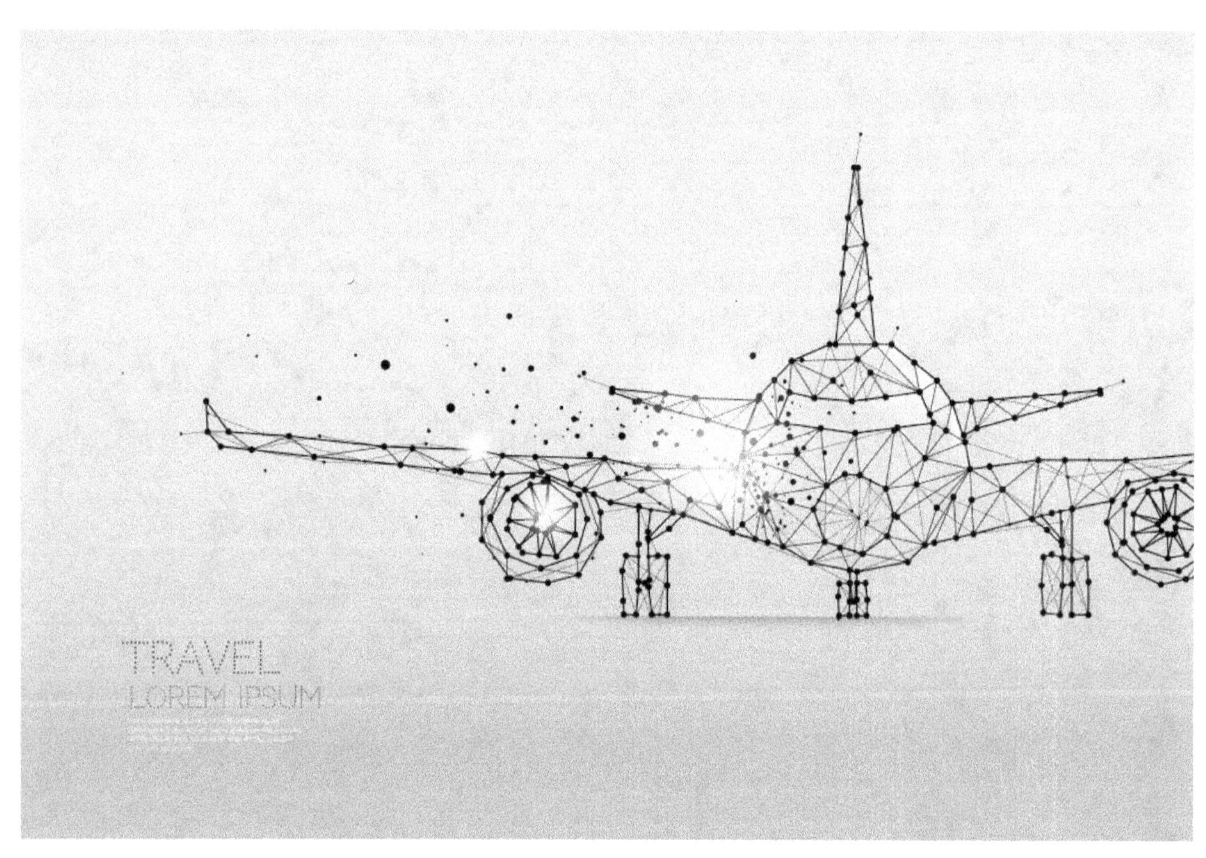

TRAVEL
LOREM IPSUM

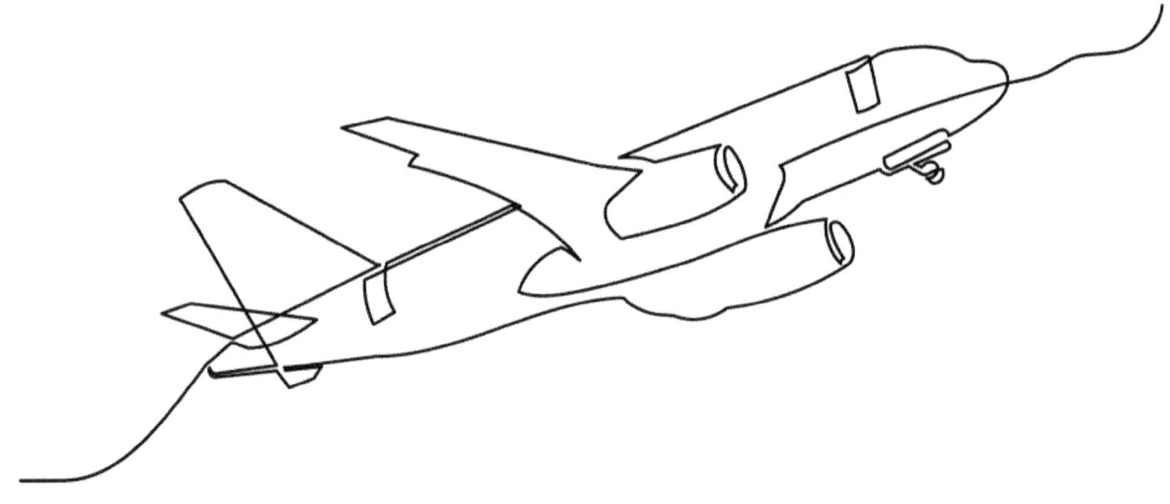